Based on original by Jonathan Weber

APOSTLE TO
MARY MAGDALENE

JULIE DE VERE HUNT

First published in the UK in 2018
© Julie de Vere Hunt
apostletomarymagdalene@gmail.com

© G2 Rights Ltd.   www.G2ent.co.uk
Printed and bound in Europe
ISBN 978-1-78281-4610

The views in this book are those of the author but they are general views only and readers are urged to consult the relevant and qualified specialist for individual advice in particular situations. G2 Entertainment Limited hereby exclude all liability to the extent permitted by law of any errors or omissions in this book and for any loss, damage or expense (whether direct or indirect) suffered by a third party relying on any information contained in this book.

All our best endeavours have been made to secure copyright clearance for every photograph used but in the event of any copyright owner being overlooked please go to www.g2ent.co.uk where you will find all relevant information.

Cover image based on an original painting by Jan van Scorel of Mary Magdalene (ca.1530)

CONTENTS

ACKNOWLEDGEMENTS

To my parents, Jean and Michael Adams, for encouraging me from cradle to adulthood - the sky was never the limit!

I am grateful for your love, support and the many financial sacrifices you made - you certainly put your children first and were a great role model for me. I couldn't have asked for a better childhood.

To my nearly twin, Edward; you have literally been there for me since the day I was born! You have supported and helped me more times than I can remember - thank you!

I have been so blessed - so many people have helped me on my journey and it is impossible to name them all here. You know who you are and I am very grateful.

To Magic Martin, who helped unleash my creative juices (and a lot more besides!)

To Ratu Bagus, who has taught me so much about myself. Thank you for your love, patience and words of wisdom.

To Ratu's wife, Nikki, who encouraged me in the early years at the ashram and has provided an invaluable bridge between east and west for Ratu's mission. Nikki also gave me that book that got the ball rolling...

To all my shaking friends in Bali and the UK, particularly my shaking family at Avebury. For listening to my trials and tribulations at our weekly group and keeping me on the not so straight and narrow!

To my publisher, Jules Gammond for helping me to get this book out into the world.

To Kay, for giving me the idea in the first place. If I achieve nothing else, my book was the first book you read for fun!

To my children, Daisy, Bella and Felix, who amaze and inspire me every single day. You taught me about unconditional love and your wise words mean more than all the books I have read!

To my husband Peter, my rock, my King. You make everything seem possible...

I have loved you before, I love you now and I will love you again.

PROLOGUE

"I have no special talents. I am only passionately curious".
Albert Einstein (1879-1955)

7.35am Tuesday 6th February

Expect nothing and await everything...

These were the first words that came to me as I sat down with my pen... and then

Mary Magdalene - why me?

I hear a voice inside, guiding me, encouraging me - is it her?

I think so... Why do I doubt myself so much?

Three times I have been told (by psychics) I will be a great writer...

Fear of failure?

That is ego - self - need it for this life in the body but best keep it in check...

It is the time of feminine power and Mary's voice needs to be heard!

Just sit with a pen and Mary will write the words - trust!

Mary was written out of history, by men, portrayed as a prostitute!

She was highly educated; before she met Jesus she trained at an order in Egypt in astronomy, mathematics, sacred geometry, philosophy and healing.

She was the power behind the throne.

It is time people knew!

Jesus was a figurehead.

A man because no one at the time would have believed a woman....

She was his strength, his love, his everything...

She stayed with him until the end, and beyond... Faithful...

I can't see her but I hear her and she wants me to write about her...

But why me? Others have already...

I don't know... I just have to trust!

Mary has been around me for a few years now - I don't see her but others have.

She is pink energy - she showed up in a photo I took in Avebury in January 2018 - it happens to be the 'feminine' stone!

An orb surrounded by pink energy!

The colour pink represents the heart chakra. Love and compassion.

The qualities of *Mary Magdalene.*

I have many doubts, but I feel this is my destiny, my contribution to help raise consciousness at this time.

I don't feel I can do this on my own, but I don't have to - there are many guides and light beings happy to help me, who want this 'story'/message out there...

I love Jesus.

I cannot imagine how painful it would have been for her to watch her beloved suffer and die on the cross.

They knew they had no future together on Earth - that was their destiny.

I have always had a strong connection with Jesus - I feel I must have been part of his group - an Essene.

I always see him in my heart meditations smiling at me, telling me what I already know. He is my counsellor, friend, who always answers my questions and petty dramas with love and patience...

And now I hear another voice, a female one, which my core tells me is Mary.

More gentle, but strong.

Persistent, but patient...

She must be patient, she has waited over 2000 years to be heard!

Not for her sake but for ours!

Our world is becoming more advanced technologically but more violent...

It is not an easy time to be on the spiritual path but a walk in the park compared to what Mary and Jesus went through so I smile and carry on!

I worry I don't know what to write and yet I hear her all the time - I just have to listen.

Mary is much cleverer than me - I am confident she will inform me 'drip by drip' so I don't get overwhelmed by the whole process.

Thank you for your trust in me...

I do not feel worthy. I am an Oxfordshire housewife with no writing credentials - there are lots of great writers out there.... this is the mind of course putting up a strong fight to stop this - but why?

Because the way forward is self-empowerment with love...

We do not need to be ruled by anyone but ourselves!

7.20am Wednesday 7th February

During my heart meditation this morning I felt total immersed in pink!

I could not see it but I could feel it!

Warm, cosy, loving - like I felt when I was comforted by my mother as a child.

But there was also this glorious sense of I AM and being able to achieve absolutely anything! Has to be Mary...

She is answering my self-doubt and questions about the form/plot of this book.

I have realised it doesn't matter...

It is not written *by* me but *through* me...

What an honour!

The empowerment of women!

Very topical with the anniversary of the women's vote and suffragettes...

Do you know where the most number of female politicians in the world are?

Rwanda, Africa.

Surprising. Presumably because the men got slaughtered in that awful civil war.

If we all came from the I AM how much easier would this drama called life be?

Glastonbury Abbey

Mary Magdalene spent some time there and I have never been!

I am being called! Mary wants to show me something...

7.30am Thursday 8th February

Glastonbury was awesome!

Parked in Magdalene Street!

We went round the Abbey, the Chalice Well and the Tor, but didn't feel her presence at all!

I stumbled upon a second hand book shop and bought two books on Mary Magdalene - I have this unquenchable thirst to read as much about her as I can...

Maybe it's procrastination, or a deep desire to be imbued with her spirit.

But I already am!

When I go into my heart it is now a blaze of pink! It must be her!

Mary is where the heart is. In my heart, in Avebury, the heart of England!

Trust and let go!

I am not alone...

Women are standing up all over the world claiming their equal rights - Tesco workers insisting on equal pay, and the BBC!

It is becoming an epidemic!

7.40am Friday 9th February

All will be well...

It is as it should be...

Go inside to see the illusion - it is perfect in your heart - create your world from there instead of trying to make yourself happy from distractions on the outside.

So obvious...

Focus on creative pursuits - painting, writing, music, cooking with love for your family - all things you love doing!

My body resonates like a tuning fork when I hear a truth from my inner voice

Test if it is true for you - we are all unique and different!

We must all take responsibility for our own truth - not rely on others - especially not the media and people in authority.

Better to seek counsel from a child - they are unlikely to obscure the truth!

Look at the world with a child!

Feel the sense of wonder which we have lost!

The beauty is still there...

We are in such a hurry we miss so much!

Slow down and turn on all your senses - eyes, ears, smell, touch and 'inner knowing'

Gnosis - inner knowing - trust it more and believe in yourself!

Write that book, quit the job you don't like - if you are content you won't need much!

Live from the heart

If you live from the heart you can only respond with love...

So, after three days of "automatic writing" in the early morning, this book was conceived...

Note: The words *in italics* are my "inner voice"

INTRODUCTION

"Reality is merely an illusion, albeit a very persistent one."
Albert Einstein

Around 10 years ago a friend gave me a copy of Kathleen McGowan's book 'The Expected One'. I was totally gripped. I felt I was actually there in Jerusalem - it was like a waking dream - I could feel the dust on my feet, the smells of the city, as I frantically made my way through the crowds in the streets of Jerusalem.

Mary Magdalene comes to me in meditation, in my dreams, she is apparently around me when I practice shaking yoga...

She has been in exile for over 2000 years, but thanks to Dan Brown's book 'The Da Vinci Code', she has been brought back into public awareness.

Scholars such as Margaret Starbird have spent decades researching the Gospels in an attempt to put the record straight and we can remember her as the great woman she was.

Now we have entered the Age of Aquarius Mary Magdalene has stepped forward to help us embrace our feminine power and restore the balance of Masculine and Feminine in all of us.

I am no wordsmith - Mary Magdalene is my guide; without her I would not have found the courage to write this.

There is little recorded fact about Mary Magdalene... but then most of history is based on oral tradition and legend. The written word is known to be subject to the bias of the author...

I have stood on the shoulders of giants; cherry-picked ideas that leapt out of the page at me, overlaid with my own personal experiences, to give you an A-Z of Mary Magdalene. I touch on quantum science to suggest how information can be accessed in meditation and dreams as these are invaluable sources.

I am an apostle (messenger) to Mary Magdalene; hopefully a bridge between spirit, science and you dear reader.

Some of the information in this book my sound incredible to some of you, but only what we don't understand is perceived as magic!

It is my belief that the answers lie within quantum science, that this is where science and spirituality will converge.

It is only you who can decide what is true for you...

A
is for
THE AGE OF AQUARIUS

The Age of Aquarius is not part of astronomy.

It is an astrological age, which occurs because of a real motion of Earth known as the 'precession of the equinoxes'.

The cycle lasts for around 26,000 years and there are 12 constellations of the Zodiac. So, roughly every 2,150 years, the sun's position at the time of the vernal equinox moves in front of a new Zodiac constellation.

Astrologers believe that an astrological age affects humanity.

We have moved from the Age of Pisces into the Age of Aquarius, although there is some debate as to the precise timing of this transition.

Both the Aquarian Age and the Mayan Great Cycle appear to have begun around 2012.

Scientists today confirmed the galactic alignment as the Maya predicted,

"There's no question that one of the great cycles of the traditional ancient Mayan calendar comes to a completion of its count at that time in 2012" says E.C. Krupp, Director of the Griffith Observatory in Los Angeles, California.

The Maya calculated over 2,000 years ago that this alignment would occur on December 21, 2012.

The Mayans recorded this time as a 'great window of opportunity for spiritual growth'.

Traditionally, the Age of Aquarius is associated with electricity, computers, democracy, freedom, humanitarianism, idealism, modernization and philanthropy.

More specifically, the age of equality between the Masculine and Feminine.

The Age of Aquarius is causing great turmoil as everything with Piscean values is being exposed or unravelling; governments, corporations, individuals, and even personal relationships.

The Age of Aquarius points to the direction of our own evolution in consciousness.

We are being asked to make a choice.

We can cling to the old outdated values or adopt the new evolving ones.

For this shift to occur, it is similar to a birthing process. It is uncomfortable and the world appears chaotic - it can feel like we are going backwards - many technological advances but violence increasing also.

Fortunately we are not on our own.

We are being helped by ascended masters and mistresses...

It is time to understand that WE are the spiritual masters we have been waiting for!

Mary Magdalene has been called to assist us, like a midwife, to support this process, the merging of the opposites, the masculine and the feminine.

These two energies within each of us will once again work together to know God.

They will bring messages from the Divine to manifestation in the world.

In a new consciousness everything will be given on demand to meet a need.

Aware individuals will not conceive of lack.

What we give out of love, grows, not diminishes.

We will become spiritual beings having a human experience instead of human beings having a worldly experience.

Spirit and matter will merge and function as one.

This is for all women and men, as we all have the Sacred Feminine and Sacred Masculine within us.

The Feminine brings life energy, love, aliveness, wisdom, faith, receptivity to the Divine, feeling and inclusiveness.

The Masculine brings insight, understanding, awareness, direction attaining goals and carrying out the Divine plan.

The Feminine (receiver of divine inspiration) and Masculine (acting out the Divine plan in the world) will unite as one unit, unquestioning, without altering messages from the Divine...

The Indigo, Crystal and Rainbow children are here to help us incorporate the Age of Aquarius values. These children possess increased spiritual sensitivity and are committed to the new values; they are not happy with the world as it is now!

Change always starts with the individual.

Synergistic efforts of the individual will change collective consciousness.

So make your personal choices carefully; a move towards the Divine and the 'new' values does have a positive effect on collective consciousness of Mother Earth.

Trust me. Once the synergistic ball starts to roll, it will be unstoppable!

In the words of Margaret Mead, American anthropologist:

"Never doubt that a small group of thoughtful, committed people can change the world. Indeed, it is the only thing that ever has."

A is for AKASHIC RECORDS

"Dreams are illustrations for the book your soul is writing."
Marsha Norman

So what exactly are the Akashic Records and what have they got to do with Mary Magdalene?

"Akashic" comes from the Sanskrit word "akasa" which means sky or ether.

Akashic Records date back to the Old Testament and early Buddhist writings but were written about extensively in the 19th century by Rudolph Steiner and Edgar Cayce.

The Akashic Records are an endless expanse of vibrating consciousness that is both our personal and collective truth. A great, invisible library in the sky!

All the mysteries of life: yours, mine, the eternity of life from before life began and will go on long after the world as we know it disappears...

From ancient wisdom to quantum physics not yet understood.

Although Mary Magdalene is mentioned in the Bible more than any other woman we still know very little about her.

She is concealed behind a shroud of myth, supposition and mystery.

But her life story is in the Akashic Records. Everybody's is!

On a personal level, they hold information from your eternal history; past, present and future. It may be an important part of your spiritual path which past lives are influencing in this life.

The Akashic Records contain information that is both fixed and evolving.

Fixed information is generally spiritual truths. For example, the story of Mary Magdalene.

Almost everything else evolves and changes, and as change occurs, so do the records.

I had heard of the Akashic Records but did not realize how accessible they were to each and every one of us.

Sandra Taylor's book 'The Akashic Records' demystifies them and explains simple techniques for accessing them.

We have the power to scan the records, view the past, the future - the sky is not the limit!

As you scan these past records, you will see patterns still influencing you today but amazingly you can change these records and shift present patterns in order to resolve a problem facing you in the here and now.

For example, I have always been a really bad loser. As a child with three brothers, my competitive spirit was put down to this family dynamic and tolerated by my parents (who are not competitive at all!)

My mother would quote tennis player Fred Perry

"Show me a good loser - never a winner!"

But as an adult with three children of my own, it was somewhat embarrassing when I couldn't even play Monopoly with my family!

I played competitive golf for many years and it was a form of mental torture.

Winning provided temporary relief and losing was just horrible!

I decided to follow the instructions in Sandra Taylor's book for the 'Sacred Temple' meditation to see if anything came up.

As I viewed the 'screen', I 'saw' myself as a Roman slave having to compete in Gladiator style games. I was literally competing for my life! Winning was just a stay of execution. Losing meant death!

It was extraordinary...

I then repeated a releasing affirmation:

"I bless the past and let it go. I am free"

The sense of relief was massive.

I am not such a bad loser now but I have stopped playing golf competitively - it is not fun for me!

Meditation, deep breathing and affirmations help you tune in to the Akashic Records.

Akashic Record guidance increases when you keep an open mind and focus on living out of your heart rather than your mind.

I write affirmations by my bed on post-it notes which I glance at before I go to sleep

"My heart and mind are open to the wisdom of the Akashic Realm."

Lots of ideas for this book come to me when I wake up in the middle of the night, presumably when my subconscious is allowed to speak!

Dreams are a powerful way to open the records and receive inspiration so keep a journal by your bed.

Paul McCartney was troubled and had a dream in which his (deceased) mother Mary came to give him advice.

The song that came out of that dream was 'Let it Be', a song that has been an inspiration to millions of people.

B is for
BRIDE OR REPENTANT SINNER?

"Great spirits have always encountered violent opposition from mediocre minds." Albert Einstein

So what do we know about Mary Magdalene?

Mary Magdalene is named after a place *Magdala* which suggests she was not married. *Magdala* is derived from the Hebrew word *Migdal* which means 'fortress' or 'tower'.

She was a Jewish woman of independent means and after Jesus 'cures' her of her affliction she joins him as one of his followers and helps to fund his mission.

We first hear of her in the Bible when Jesus casts out the 'seven demons' from her.

In Luke 7, an unnamed woman anoints Jesus's feet and is referred to as a *sinner*. This is assumed to be Mary Magdalene and seems to be where she gains her reputation as a prostitute, although in those days a *sinner* would not necessarily have implied this.

It was one of the pillars of Judaism that a Jewish male would be married by the age of 20.

According to Margaret Starbird, there are two events in the New Testament which suggest Mary Magdalene could have been the bride of Jesus.

The anointing of Jesus with the alabaster jar of ointment and the reunion in the garden after the crucifixion.

According to the Gospel of Mark, the anointing took place at the house of Simon in Bethany; "there came a woman with an alabaster jar of ointment, genuine nard of great value, and breaking the alabaster jar, she poured it on his head" (Mark 14:3).

The disciples were aghast at the waste of such valuable ointment but Jesus admonished them replying

"She has anointed me in advance for my burial. Truly I tell you, wherever the good news is proclaimed in the whole world, what she has done will be told in remembrance of her." (Mark 14:3-9)

In John's gospel, Jesus requests that Mary keep the remainder of the precious ointment she used to anoint him for the day of his burial.

Messiah means anointed and in early history anointing became identified with the nuptial ceremony of the *hieros gamos* - the sacred marriage uniting the royal priestess representing the Goddess, her land, and her people, with her chosen King.

Early Gnostic theologians believe that Jesus, as Christ the Logos (Divine Order or Word), and Magdalene, as Christ the Sophia (Wisdom) together form the Christos, the Anointed One.

This sacred relationship echoes other divine couplings such as Radha-Krishna, Shiva-Shakti, Adonis-Venus or Osiris-Isis.

"The Saviour loved Mary Magdalene more than all the disciples. And he kissed her often on her mouth. The rest of the disciples were jealous of her. They asked and said to him

'Why do you love her more than all of us?'

The Saviour answered and said to them

'Why do I not love you like her?" (Gospel of Phillip)

Mary Magdalene was one of the *myrrhophores,* the female ointment bearers who came to mourn the death of Jesus and anoint his corpse in final preparation for his burial.

Corpses were considered unclean under Jewish law, left to the female family members to prepare the body for burial.

The three Marys undertook this task; Mary Magdalene, Mary mother of Jesus and Mary Salome.

"But Mary Magdalene stood weeping outside the tomb. As she wept, she bent over into the tomb, and she saw two angels in white sitting where the body of Jesus had been lying, one at the head and the other at the feet.

They said to her, "Woman, why are you weeping?"

She said to them

"They have taken away my Lord and I do not know where they have laid him." (John 20:11-13)

Jesus approaches her and at first she mistakes him for the gardener. He also asks why she is crying and her tears turn to joy as she realizes who he is.

Their reunion is sadly short-lived and Jesus tells Mary to go and tell the disciples that He is risen, fulfilling her role as *Apostle to the Apostles.*

"Mary stood up, greeted them all, and said to her brothers,

'Do not weep or grieve or be in doubt, for his grace will be with you all and will protect you. Rather let us praise his greatness, for he has prepared us and made us truly human" (Gospel of Mary)

Jesus transmitted secret teachings to Mary Magdalene that were withheld from the other apostles.

Peter said to Mary: "Tell us whatever you remember of any words he told you which we have not yet heard".

"Mary said to them: 'I will speak to you of that which has not been given to you to hear. I had a vision of the Teacher, and I said to him 'Lord, I see you now in this vision'.

And he answered, 'You are blessed, for the sight of me does not disturb you. There where is the nous, lies the treasure." (Gospel of Mary)

So, through means of the nous or *divine intelligence,* Mary

Magdalene understood Jesus in his new state of being.

Starbird makes a comparison with the Old Testament book 'The Song of Songs' - a bride mourning the sacrificed bridegroom echoing ancient legends of sacrificed kings?

Saint Mary Magdalene is certainly recognized by the Church as someone who loved Jesus very much, was faithful to the end and beyond, and the first person to see Jesus after the Resurrection.

The Church does not accept Mary Magdalene was the bride of Jesus.

The jury is still out - they will never agree!

There is no written evidence but it is all in the *Akashic Records*!

We will return to this.

C is for CELLULAR MEMORY

"Logic will get you from A-Z; imagination will get you everywhere."
Albert Einstein

Mainstream science tells us the part of our body that stores and recalls events that occur in our life is in our brain.

Well it is, but memory is also held in each and every cell in your body.

It is called *cellular memory*.

Every cell in your body holds information on all levels of your being, physically, emotionally, mentally and spiritually.

This cellular memory is constantly updated from your past lives, this life, right up until the present time (overlap with *Akashic Records* here).

Your cells contain DNA which is the blueprint for the complete design of your body and characterises who you are.

DNA that you inherited from your family and all your memories from this life and past lives.

When you go through a traumatic experience, your body suppresses the overwhelming situation by storing the memory in your cells. This is commonly called shock and is self- protection for the body.

Sometime later you release this from the cells by crying, shaking or trembling.

However, sometimes these memories are never released because they are just too traumatic.

They can cause an imbalance in the physical body manifesting in a physical or emotional illness.

You can access these held memories in many cases through meditation, but in more severe cases you may need help from a trained therapist or counsellor .

The most interesting case for *cellular memory* is the numerous reports of organ recipients who later experienced changes in personality traits, taste for food, music, activities and even sexual preferences.

These memories reside deep within our cells.

In Dr Bruce Lipton's book *"The Biology of Belief"* he talks about the phenomena of transplant organ recipients adopting characteristics of the donor.

Claire Sylvia was astonished when she developed a taste for beer, chicken nuggets and motor cycles after her heart-lung transplant.

Sylvia talked to the donor's family and discovered she had the heart of an eighteen year old motorcycle enthusiast who loved chicken nuggets and beer!

In her book *"A Change of Heart"*, Sylvia outlines her personal transformational experiences as well as similar experiences of other members of her transplant support group.

The accuracy of memories that accompany these transplants is beyond chance or coincidence.

Heart surgeon Dr Paul Pearsall agrees with this.

He states that according to his study of patients who have received transplant organs, particularly hearts, it is not uncommon for new memories, behaviour and habits associated with the donor to be transferred to the recipient.

Our memories are not only stored within our brain but in our internal organs as well.

Heart surgeon Dr Mehmet Oz operating at Columbia Presbyterian Medical Centre invited energy healer Julie Motz into the operating room during transplant surgery.

He hoped she would be able to help to allay a patient's fear and anxiety.

She did, but there was also a reduction in a patient's rejection of the new organ and increased survival rates.

Motz helps the recipient to accept the new organ and also works with the donated tissue as well.

Dr Lipton goes onto say that organ transplants offer a model not only for immortality but also for reincarnation.

Because our environment represents All That Is (God) or Source, we all represent a small part of the whole... a small part of God.

We are all connected...

D

DIVINE FEMININE

"I must be willing to give up what I am in order to become what I will be" Albert Einstein

We need to reclaim the Divine or Sacred Feminine both for our individual spirituality and for the well- being of our planet.

Our ecological devastation points to a culture that has forgotten the sacredness of the earth and the Divine Mother, as well as denied the feminine's deep understanding of the wholeness and interconnectedness of all of life.

So what does it mean to reclaim the Divine Feminine?

How can we feel it in our bodies and in our daily life?

Every woman knows this mystery in the cycles of her body, which are linked to the greater rhythms of life, the cycles of the moon.

The feminine carries a natural understanding of the connectedness of life.

She instinctively knows how to respond to the needs of her children, how she feels for their well-being even when they are not physically present.

And in her body she carries the greatest mystery, the potential to give birth; to bring the light of a soul into this world.

The feminine is the matrix of creation.

Regardless of whether an individual woman has the physical

experience of giving birth, she shares in this primal mystery and is empowered by it.

Our culture's focus on a disembodied, transcendent God has left women bereft, denying them the sacredness of this simple mystery of divine love.

This patriarchal denial affects not only women, but life itself.

We cut our world off from the source that alone can heal, nourish and transform it.

Of course men also have a need to relate to the Divine Feminine, to be nourished by her inner and outer presence.

Many times before the world has been through an ecological crisis, and the world soul carries within her the memories and wisdom we need.

But we need to listen...

If we continue to see it as a problem we need to fix with more advanced technology, we will just compound the crisis.

So Divine Feminine energy is an elevated, ego-diminished, non-judgemental and non-harming state of Being that transcends the human mind.

It is a state of awareness that is connected to the wisdom of the heart, to natural and divine laws, and to a loving, harmonious and peaceful life.

Both men and women have access to Divine Feminine energy. Which brings me to Mary Magdalene.

The silent power behind the throne...

The favoured disciple who Jesus shared his thoughts, doubts and sought counsel from.

Mary Magdalene is a manifestation of the feminine face of God in the female half of creation.

There are practical ways of helping us connect to Divine Feminine energy to help us in our everyday lives:

1 Feel your feelings
Feelings are emotions attached to physical sensations.

We are all tempted to run away from uncomfortable or painful feelings... But they tend to follow you!

To access divine feminine energy we need to fully feel and release our feeling without judgement.

Stagnant feelings can become held not only in the physical body, but also in the 'spiritual body' and may restrict the flow of divine feminine energy.

You need to find a safe space or group of trust-worthy friends where you can fully feel your feelings.

2 Trust your intuition
Intuition is a gift of the Divine Feminine.

Intuitive impulses come from the Heart, and are always for the Highest Good of All.

An intuitive impulse is often accompanied by signs and synchronicities in the external world.

So keep all six senses open to receive!

3 Create a sacred space
Your feminine soul energy wakes up when you create and take part in simple ritual and ceremony.

As simple as lighting a candle or incense stick before you meditate or pray.

4 Listen to your Body

Your body is an invaluable instrument for Divine Feminine truth and wisdom.

Your body will let you know when something is not right for you, not serving your highest good.

Honour and treat your body as a temple!

Eat light, breathe deep.

Get enough sleep and take exercise - you don't have to run a marathon - a walk in nature is so re-energizing.

Enjoy your sexuality!

Religion has imprinted on us women that to enjoy sex is wanton (no sex before marriage in Christianity).

Do you think God would make it so enjoyable?

Treated with respect and entered into with love it is a gift!

5 Listen to your Inner Voice

Creating regular times of stillness, quiet, meditation and contemplation activate divine feminine energy.

The inner voice is connected to your divine feminine contract with the universe.

We all have a spiritual role to fulfil here on earth and our inner voice guides us step by step.

There is no right or wrong way to practice.

It is the intention which is important.

The Divine Feminine is here for each and every one of us, waiting patiently to be called…

D is for DARK GODDESS

Dark is not "bad" or "evil".

We live in duality. Light and dark. Day and night. Male and female.

We need both. And we need a balance.

The Dark Goddess is the embodiment of the dark phase of the moon's cycle.

The Dark Goddess is associated with fertility rites, death, war, revenge...

Skills associated with her were astrology, magic, alchemy and mid-wifery.

They came under suspicion by the increasingly male dominated church, as they remain today.

In the early days of Christianity, following Jesus's teachings, women held positions such as bishops, deacons and preachers.

By the year 200 this was no longer the case!

By demonizing menstruation, childbirth and traditional herbal medicine, the Church discounted and dismissed women's powers.

Mary, mother of Jesus, with her virtues of virginity and chastity, became the female figurehead for the Church.

Mary Magdalene, denigrated as a prostitute by the Church, has become the Christian Dark Goddess, revered for her sexuality and independence.

She is the independently wealthy woman of the Gospels, who is not under control of a father, husband or son.

Black Virgin shrines exist in at least fifty churches dedicated to Mary Magdalene, mostly in France.

While most of us may assume that Black Madonnas are depictions of the Virgin Mary holding the child Jesus, Starbird believes some of the Black Madonna statues depict Mary Magdalene with her child, the fruit of her relationship with Jesus.

Starbird recognises Mary Magdalene as the latest manifestation of the Dark Goddess.

Starbird also believes some of the greatest artists such as Botticelli and Da Vinci honoured the Dark Goddess by hiding her symbols in their paintings.

So how is all this relevant to us today?

To express and celebrate the Dark Goddess as she was originally understood.

We should delight in our bodies, our emotions, our sexuality, our independence and our power.

The Dark Goddess is a deep well of wisdom and fearlessness!

E

is for
EGYPT

"There is freedom only when there is freedom from the known."
Krishnamurti

So we believe Mary Magdalene was an educated, independently wealthy Jewish woman born in the Galilean town of Magdala.

She was reputedly trained in herbal medicine, astronomy, philosophy, mathematics (geomatra), meditation and tantra.

Margaret Starbird has spent decades studying the Gospels and Mary Magdalene. In her book "Bride in Exile", she poses the theory that Mary Magdalene trained through the temple of Isis as a high priestess, mainly in healing and blessing work.

She would have been trained in the highest art of serving the Divine through Sacred Relationship. She would have been taught to relate to all of life as the play of God; to see all the parts of herself as holy and sacred - physical, emotional, mental and ethereal and spiritual bodies.

These skills would have served her well in her role alongside Jesus.

But there are no hard facts. Even the Bible which the Church hangs its hat on is a series of eye witness events. The Gospels were written from AD 70-95, nearly 40 years after Jesus died.

This is why I talk about the Akashic Records, cellular memory, kinesiology and meditation.

They are all ways of sourcing the Truth - mine and yours...

200 years ago electricity would have been considered witchcraft.

In fact we didn't invent electricity.

Thomas Eddison discovered it with the invention of the electric light bulb in 1879.

It was there all along, we just weren't looking in the right place!

I don't fully understand how electricity works but I accept it because I can see the results and benefits of it...

So maybe we need to change our scientific paradigms, the way we look at metaphysical phenomena?

F

FRANCE

"Only a life lived for others is a life lived worthwhile."
Albert Einstein

Catharism ("the pure ones" in Greek) was a Christian dualist or gnostic revival movement that thrived in northern Italy and southern France between the 12th and 14th centuries.

The followers were known as Cathars and suffered a prolonged period of prosecution by the Catholic Church which considered them heretics.

The idea of two Gods or principles, one being good and the other evil, was central to Cathar beliefs. The good God was the God of the New Testament and the creator of the spiritual realm, contrasted with the evil Old Testament God - creator of the physical world.

Cathars believed in reincarnation and the equality of women. If the spirit was immaterial and sexless, women were equally capable of being religious leaders. This upset the male-dominated Catholic Church.

Legends surfaced in the 12th and 13th century Cathar region in Provence, France that in AD 43, Mary Magdalene and her family sailed in a rudderless boat known as the Bark of Mary, to Marseilles in the south of France.

With her were her sister Martha and her 9 year old maid Sarah, brother Lazarus, Mary mother of Jesus and Mary Salome.

The three Mary's travelled around the south of France teaching the message of transforming Love, converting the royal family and much of the population.

The two Marys remained in a small coastal town in the Camargue now named after them: Les Saintes Maries de la Mer (Saint Marys by the sea). Lazarus went to Marseilles where he became a bishop, and Martha to Tarascon.

Mary Magdalene spent the last 20 years of her life in prayer and meditation in a mountain cave in the sacred forest of La Saint Baume. Reputedly her only sustenance was the Holy Eucharist, which she received on a daily basis from the angels. During her waning years, the angels descended from heaven and transported her to a secret location. There she feasted on celestial harmonies and witnessed the Rapture.

The Cathars believed Mary Magdalene was the wife of Jesus and Sarah was her daughter. The Catholic church was not happy about these rumours about Mary Magdalene and in 1239 formed the Inquisition to stamp them out by brutally murdering thousands of Cathars.

Despite this, the legends survived and Mary Magdalene continued to be widely worshipped.

In 1279, Charles, nephew of King Louis IX of France, reputedly discovered Mary Magdalene's remains at the church of St Maximum in Provence.

The King, a devotee, transferred the relics to the church's crypt in 1280, where they still are today. Her skull is in a gold reliquary and other relics in a marble sarcophagus.

Every year the feast day of Mary Magdalene is celebrated on the 22 July in St Maximum much to the delight of her followers.

Mary Magdalene lives on, at least in France.

This poem was found a few years ago in the crypt of St Maximum:-

"Mary Magdalene, Beautiful Saint of Provence.

You, who was healed and saved by Jesus, return us to the splendour of our souls and the Beauty of God.

You, faithful disciple and woman who sees and hears, anchor our hearts in the word of Life. Help us to hear, to hold and to put into practice the teachings of Christ our Lord and Saviour.

You, who have known tears and have spread the perfume of Love, comfort all those who suffer, pouring forth your balm to soothe our souls.

You, loyal servant at the Cross and Tomb. Allow us the Grace of Hope during our many struggles, Strength during our trials, Faith in Eternal Life at the moment of death.

You were the first to see the Risen Lord, and deservedly so.

You received the mission to tell his disciples you had seen him.

Make of us, honourable and courageous witnesses of the Risen Christ in His Eternal Glory."

Anon

G

GLASTONBURY

"The most beautiful thing we can experience is the mysterious."
Albert Einstein

Glastonbury was the earliest Christian monastic site in Britain and by Domesday it was the wealthiest abbey in England.

In 1601 the Vatican librarian, Cesare Baronius, recorded that Joseph of Arimathea (uncle of Jesus) first came to Marseilles and then on to the West of England in AD 35, nine years before the Magdalene voyage.

Joseph and his twelve missionaries were greeted with cordiality by King Arviragus of Siluria. The King granted Joseph twelve hides of Glastonbury land - about 1,440 acres.

In AD 63-64 they built a unique little wattle church of St Mary on a scale of the ancient Tabernacle of Moses. These grants to Joseph remained holdings of free land for many centuries and are recorded in the Domesday Book of 1086: the church of Glastonbury.

The chapel of St Mary was the first above ground Christian church in the world.

The dedication was to St Mary (generally presumed to be Jesus's mother). But as confirmed in the 12th century Chronica of Matthew Paris, AD 63 was the very year Mary Magdalene died at La Sainte Baume.

Legend also relates that Joseph of Arimathea, the three Marys and other followers of Jesus arrived at Glastonbury sometime after being exiled from the Holy Land.

Glastonbury's sacred sites include the Abbey, the Tor and the Chalice Well.

The Tor is a Celtic term meaning *A Thin Place* where the barrier between the earth and spirit world is narrow.

Spiritual reality allegedly impinges into material reality at these locations and one "senses" a connection to the spiritual nature at the core of reality - associated with a feeling of peace, wonder and awe.

The Tor tower is the remains of a 14th century church dedicated to St Michael.

The Chalice Well is one of Britain's oldest wells, situated at the base of the Tor. This is where Joseph of Arimathea is believed to have placed the chalice that had caught the blood of Jesus at the crucifixion.

The water is believed to have healing properties.

Christian mythology also suggests the red of the water represents the rusty nails used at the crucifixion.

Joseph brought a hawthorn staff which he planted on Wearyall Hill in Glastonbury. The staff is thought to have grown into the Holy Thorn Tree which you can see today.

It flowers twice a year at Christmas and Easter to recall the birth and death of Jesus, and the bringing of Christianity to our islands.

Each year a sprig from another Holy thorn tree in the town is cut for the Queen, a tradition which dates back more than 100 years.

The Queen places the sprig on her dining room table on Christmas Day.

HOLY GRAIL

"A man should look for what is, and not what he thinks should be."
Albert Einstein

People searching for ancient drinking cups and chalices have studied art and folklore for clues as to the whereabouts of the vessel that once contained the blood of Christ.

Clearly there must have been an actual cup from which Jesus drank at the Passover meal, but is that the drinking cup of the Holy Grail legend?

Margaret Starbird suggests that the Holy Grail was not an artefact but the blood royal (sang raal) of the Davidic kings of Israel. She further points out that the term sang raal spelt differently - as san graal means Holy Grail...

Royal blood lines are not carried around in a chalice.

The sacred container could have been Mary Magdalene, along with any child born of her union with Jesus.

Starbird thinks Mary Magdalene was taken to Alexandria in Egypt after the crucifixion by Joseph Arimathea - the Romans were hunting down Jesus' followers and Joseph would have been concerned about Mary's safety.

My body (i.e. cellular memory) confirms this.

This would also explain why there is no further mention of Mary Magdalene in the Gospels. She was no longer there!

47

Mary Magdalene stayed here until AD 43 when she left for France with her inner circle.

The name Sarah means *princess* in Hebrew - could 9 year old Sarah, the child on the boat, be Mary Magdalene's daughter? Well, the dates are right...

My cellular memory also confirms this!

And the Cathars believe this.

Every year, at the folk festival in Saintes Maries de la Mer, locals dress little Sarah's statue in layers of multi-coloured silk and several thousand pilgrims sing hymns blessing Saint Sarah. Truth is often stranger than fiction...

I

is for
ICONS

"When you change the way you look at things, the things to look at change." Max Planck

No one knows what Mary Magdalene looked like - all we have is art...

The pre-Raphaelites, formed in the nineteenth century by Dante Gabriel Rosetti and friends, were greatly inspired by the legends of Mary Magdalene and the Grail. Although active for a period of only ten years or so, they were prolific.

Mary Magdalene is often shown with a skull, a cup or chalice, an alabaster jar, a book, and a red egg.

The shape and function of both *cups* and *skulls* call to mind the cauldron and the alembic (the glass container used by alchemists), both vessels in which transformation and metamorphosis occur.

The cup also carries the rich symbolism of sustenance, holy blood, and healing waters, all intimately connected with goddess energies.

In Christian times, churches and hermitages dedicated to women saints would often be found near a sacred well or spring.

Furthermore, *the skull* is believed to represent our mortality, bringing a compassionate quality to our interaction with others, as well as an awareness of the world as transitory.

The *book* signifies her role as guardian of the mysteries imparted by Jesus and of wisdom in general.

The *alabaster jar* relates to the scene in the New Testament, when Mary Magdalene anoints Jesus with expensive oil from a vessel. Anointing with costly oil was a king making gesture - the word *Messiah* means anointed one. Incidentally, this is one of only four events recorded in all four gospels - so presumably it was important.

The *jar* also suggests Mary Magdalene's roles as priestess and healer.

Finally, the *red egg* originates from a story where Mary Magdalene was dining with Emperor Tiberius Caesar and his dinner guests recounting Jesus's resurrection. As she sat there holding an egg, she pronounced "Christ is Risen!" consistent with her role as witness to the Risen Lord.

Caesar ridiculed her, saying that a man could no more rise from the dead than the egg in her hand could turn red. The egg immediately turned crimson, and to this day red eggs are an important part of the Orthodox Christian Easter holiday.

But Mary Magdalene wasn't finished with Tiberius yet. She let him know it was Pontius Pilate, governor of Judea, who had ordered the execution of Jesus.

This prompted Tiberius to send Pilate to Gaul, effectively in exile, where he remained until he died.

J

is for

JUNG

"Your vision will become clear when you can look into your own heart. Who looks outside dreams; who looks inside awakes."
Carl Gustav Jung (1875-1961)

Carl Gustav Jung was a Swiss psychiatrist and psychoanalyst who founded analytical psychology.

Jung's work on himself and his patients convinced him that our purpose in life is to discover and fulfil our deep innate potential.

Jung's view of the symbols, myths and metaphors of the Gnostics inspired his life's work.

"All my work, all my creative activity, has come from those initial fantasies... everything that I accomplished in later life was already contained in them... although at first only in the forms of emotions and images".

Based on his study of Christianity, Hinduism, Buddhism, Gnosticism and Taoism, this journey of transformation is at the mystical heart of all religions.

To meet the Self and the Divine.

*"I have treated many hundreds of patients. Among those over 35, there has not been **one** whose problem was not finding a religious/spiritual outlook on life".*

Jung said all of us are both male (Logos) and female (Eros) formed in the image of God.

Jung went onto say that *enlightenment* comes from union and integration of Logos (logic) and Eros (intuition).

It flows from the union and integration of both ways of knowing - logic and intuition.

In other words Divine or Sacred union of the male and female.

In Jung's "Answer to Job", he stresses the need to restore the *human* bride of the human Jesus to our collective experience.

The equality of the couple - *"requires to be metaphysically anchored in the figure of a divine woman, the Bride of Christ."*

Jung says that just as the human Christ cannot be replaced by an institution, the Church, the bride needs to also be in human form.

A woman - his Domina counterpart - who represents her people.

Mary Magdalene

Jung goes onto say that recognising both the evil and the Divine Presence within ourselves is necessary for the healing of the human race.

K

is for
KINESIOLOGY

"You don't have a soul, you are a soul, you have a body."
C S Lewis

I have been seeing a kinesiologist in Newbury for two years, known affectionately by his clients as "Magic Martin".

Kinesiology is a gentle healing technique which improves the balance of an individual . An assessment is made through muscle testing; tension in the muscles reveals blocked energy in the body. The body is then stimulated into its self-healing modality.

There are many different types of kinesiology - Martin uses the Professional Kinesiology Practice (PKP)

In addition, Martin is an applied metaphysicist.

Metaphysics was coined by the Greek philosopher Aristotle (384BC-322BC). Metaphysics is the study of the true nature of reality, experience and who we really are. Arguably, it is at the root of all philosophy.

Reality is how we perceive our physical life experience.

Perception and belief are the primary mechanisms that control our biology. So misperceptions and false beliefs can disrupt our genes. This in turn may lead to dysfunction and dis-ease, which is why thought becomes a prominent contributor to our state of health.

Metaphysical principles operate at a deeper level of awareness than we previously perceived as purely physical.

Using kinesiology as a tool, a PKP practitioner applies metaphysical principles to health and well-being by affecting change in the human psyche, and in so doing illness can have no place in the human body or mind.

Human beings are able to function at their optimum level of efficiency. This can also lead to developing intuition, receiving inner guidance and experiencing inner peace.

All levels are positively affected - emotional, physical and spiritual.

From Dr Bruce Lipton's book *"The Biology of Belief"*

"The character of our lives is determined not by our genes but our responses to environmental signals. Your perspective is always limited by how much you know and what you believe. Expand your knowledge and you will transform your beliefs, your genes and ultimately your health."

You can also tap into your cellular memory using kinesiology.

There is an overlap with Akashic Records and Cellular Memory here...

Your body knows the answer to everything, albeit on a yes/no answer format.

The tested muscle stays strong for a 'yes' and goes weak for a 'no'.

Not just this lifetime, but from the past, the present and even the future!

I asked my body if I was in Egypt with Mary Magdalene, in Jerusalem at the time of Jesus and in France with the Cathars.

The answer was yes, to all three questions!

Past lives are not the focus here, but it does explain, to me anyway, why I feel so passionately about Mary Magdalene and helping to get her story out.

Sounds crazy I know...

I am not here to try and convince you - that is your choice.

I am sharing it because it was an important realisation in my journey.

So, on a personal level, to say seeing Martin has been life-changing is no under-statement, and his six week waiting list suggests I am not alone in this view.

Not only is my physical health better than ever, as I have got in touch with my Divine Feminine my creative side has been unleashed; painting, playing the piano and possibly most importantly, hearing my inner voice.

It was always there, I just wasn't listening.

Finally, I am writing the book I always wanted to write.

It feels like my life purpose and all the experiences I have had up until now have led me here...

Have you thought what yours is?

What are you waiting for?

L

LOVE AND LIGHT

"When the higher flows into the lower, it transforms the nature of the lower into that of the higher." Meister Eckhart

Love transcends form and time.

I love my mother and think of her every single day. She passed away in 2005.

I love Jesus and he died over 2000 years ago!

When I watched the film 'Mary Magdalene', a wave of emotion hit me as Mary appeared on the screen. I found myself sitting with my hands in the prayer position and tears rolling down my face!

Love comes from the heart.

The heart is the first organ to form in the human foetus.

When that heart starts to beat it creates an electromagnetic field that surrounds the heart.

Within that field are signals, energy and information, that interact with and direct the development of all the other organs, cells and tissues that will become the fully formed baby, child and adult.

The signals coming from the heart also shape the child's mind.

Babies spend an enormous amount of time 'dreaming' before they are even born.

What are these dreams made of?

Images and feelings coming from God or Source, preparing the infant to correctly perceive and function in the physical world which they will emerge and develop.

Before the child emerges from the womb, he or she is fully connected to God.

This is innocence.

It is also the state of innocence we associate with Adam and Eve before they ate the apple from the tree of knowledge of good and evil.

After birth the experience of disconnection from God begins.

If we could remember the day we were born, we would remember those first feelings of fear and imagined isolation.

But we remain connected to God throughout our entire existence, no matter what seems to happen to us in the physical world.

But as adults we must learn to reconnect *consciously.*

It *is* possible to experience Heaven on Earth.

We can *all* help to raise human consciousness and save our planet from its seemingly current course of self-destruction.

Remember we are not alone - there are many like-minded individuals who feel the same here on earth, not to mention the light beings and ascended masters in the wings just waiting to be asked to help...

Love and Light

Take a few deep breaths and connect with Mother Earth (see U for Unity Breath) Think of a place you love (beach, forest, mountains) and send your love and gratitude to the Earth. She will return it because she loves us.

Feel her love come up through the soles of your feet and permeate every cell in your body.

Allow it to fill your heart.

Now turn your attention to Father Sky. Send love to the Sun –feel the Light enter your body through the crown of your head and let it fill every cell in your body.

Focus on your heart where the *Love and Light* have now merged.

Send that fused *Love and Light* out into the world via your thoughts, intentions and actions.

If you want proof check out *"The Hidden Messages in Water"* by Dr Masaru Emoto.

He describes the ability of water to absorb, hold and even retransmit human feelings and emotions. Using high-speed photography, he found that crystals formed in frozen water reveal changes when specific thoughts and emotions are directed towards it.

He found that water from clear springs and water exposed to loving words shows brilliant, complex and colourful snowflake patterns, while polluted water and water exposed to negative thoughts form incomplete, asymmetrical patterns with dull colours.

Emoto believes that since people are 70% water, and the Earth is 70% water, we can heal our planet and ourselves by consciously expressing love and goodwill.

Your open heart is the most powerful vessel of transformation; of receiving Divine Light and empowering it with Love.

Practice until it becomes a dance, a cosmic dance, in joy...

We have to be the change we are looking to create.

M is for
MEDITATION

'Prayer is when you talk to God, meditation is when you listen to God." Anon

Meditation quietens the mind, which allows you to connect to pure presence, experiencing a state of stillness, peace, tranquillity, spaciousness and no time.

If you haven't meditated before, get a book from the library, or join a meditation group near you (it is more powerful meditating in a group and you can share your experiences).

Meditate every day.

When you have got the hang of it you can do it anywhere - in bed, in the bath, on the train - just not when you are driving a car!

It's not a chore.

It refreshes you.

It rebalances you.

Meditation is the gateway to the universe!

I am only in kindergarten and yet I have been blessed by some mind-blowing experiences!

Feelings of joy, bliss, love, compassion, forgiveness, peace dissolve my *drama of the moment* in such a gentle way....

Our world in relation to the universe/s is like a grain of sand in the desert.

And there are many deserts.

It is beyond our comprehension and experience so the mind is of little use.

So, why restrict your experience to this three dimensional earthly plane when the infinite beauty and power of your soul is waiting for you?

You can help others too...

The founder of Transcendental Meditation (TM), Maharishi Mahesh Yogi, believed individual stress led to world stress and in turn group calm led to world calm.

He proposed that if 1% of an area had people practising TM all kinds of conflict - violence, drug abuse, even traffic accidents - would decrease.

Regularly practising TM enables you to get in touch with a field that connects all things (see Z for Zero Point Field).

The TM organization called this *'Super Radiance'*; just as super radiance in the brain or in a laser creates coherence and unity, so meditation would similarly affect society.

Since 1979, a US Super Radiance group ranging in size from several hundred to 8,000 has gathered twice a day at Maharishi International University in Iowa to create greater harmony in the world.

The data is compelling. Many of the studies have been published in scientific journals, meaning they had to meet strict protocols.

Crime rates dropped until the end of the experiment. As soon as the experiment ended and the group disbanded, crime rates rose again.

Good may well be able to conquer evil after all.

We have the collective capacity to make the world a better place... No time like the present...

N

is for
NUMBERS

Gematria was a system used by the Pythagorean school of philosophers to stress the meaning of important phrases in texts.

Each letter of the Greek alphabet has a numeric value.

The Bible, written in Greek, used this form of encoding.
It is a historic way of enhancing text.

So instead of setting sacred texts to music, the ancients set them to numbers.

A word, phrase or title would carry the energy of the cosmic principle.

All the Marys are holy. M-a-r-i-a adds up to 152, a holy number, representing the sacred feminine.

The title of Mary Magdalene was h *Magdalhnh*.

Her sacred number is 153, the Holy of Holies (hieros gamos).

Her title is not a place, it was made for her and means *Tower of the Flock*, representing the people.

It equates her symbolically with the 153 fishes in the unbroken net (John 21:11), a metaphor for the Church, fishers of men and women.

It also associates her with the womb, the matrix, creativity and *vesica piscis*, 'vessel of the fish'.

These symbols were widely associated with Sophia, the goddess of wisdom and fertility in the ancient near East.

Yeshua in Hebrew is *Ihsous*; the sum of these letters is 888, the principle of resurrection and regeneration.

O
is for
ORBS

"Look deep, deep into nature, and then you will understand everything." Albert Einstein

I include this section in an attempt to explain the photo of the feminine stone in Avebury on page 10.

I first came across orbs on a visit to Ratu's ashram in Bali around 10 years ago.

The circle and the sphere are the most basic shapes in maths and physics.

No beginning and no end.

Oneness.

The circle is universally protective. They influence the human psyche.

Indian cultures understood this thousands of years ago - mandalas are still used today as meditation tools.

Orbs appear on photographs taken in low light with a flash - 'balls of light' varying in size and colour. Some of them seem to have faces....

It was years before physicist Klaus Heinemann was convinced of the existence of orbs. He and his wife, Gundi, wrote a book *"Orbs: Their Mission and Messages of Hope"*.

Sceptics claim they are dust particles or moisture on the lens surface but they are far too prevalent for that to be the case.

They have also appeared under 'clean room' conditions in a laboratory (i.e. where dust particles have been eradicated).

Orbs can also move at high speed.

Dust particles cannot!

There is video footage on youtube showing moving orbs, including videos taken at Ratu's ashram in Bali.

The Heinemanns conclude them to be *partial emanations from spirit beings'* and they are here to help us.

They believe they appear to give us a message; either for the person taking the photograph or the person being photographed.

The messages are simple, practical, affirming and helpful.

I had a beautiful experience on my last visit to Bali in November 2017.

I was having a cup of tea around 10.30pm with a good friend called T on our hotel balcony... T's twin sister Y had died two days earlier and she was worried whether she was OK. T went to the bathroom and a light in the sky caught my eye. I thought it was an aeroplane at first, but then it grew into a ball of light (orb) and started moving to the right, and then to the left.

"I think Y is here!" I called out to T.

She came rushing out and sat beside me, mouth open. Then T said

"But how do I know it is Y? Last time I saw her she was on tubes and in a coma!"

Immediately, a shaft of light (as in a matchstick man) dropped down from the orb.

"Ah, there is her body" T commented calmly... "But how do I know it is *actually* her?" she repeated.

Another orb appeared, joined to the original one, like a twin, and they danced across the sky together.

"Ah, there's me!" T said immediately.

We watched this display for around 20 minutes, too mesmerised to think about taking a photo. T was my witness.

T added "I don't know what that was, but it was very beautiful and I will remember it as long as I live".

The message was clear to me, but it wasn't meant for me!

I lay in bed that night smiling to myself, wondering if spirit beings ever got exasperated trying to communicate with us!

P
PILGRIMAGE

"The longest journey is the journey inwards." Dag Hammerskjold

The term *pilgrim* derives from the Latin word peregrinus, which means a foreigner, a stranger, or someone on a journey.

A pilgrimage, or soulful travel, is not just a physical journey, but more importantly an inner journey, a spirit renewing ritual.

Throughout the world, every culture has sacred places, where the physical meets the spiritual world and the veil is thin.

Pilgrimage can often be a gateway for a life changing experience.

As a pilgrim, you come unburdened without the constraints of ordinary life, so you are more open to experience the mysterious and miraculous.

With a sharpened focus and attention to the path, being in the present, it is possible to transform the most ordinary journey into a sacred journey, a pilgrimage.

Every sacred destination has healing miracles associated with it - spiritual and physical.

For many, physical healing is the great motivation for pilgrimage. Miracles have been associated with sacred sites where divine visions occurred, like Lourdes or Knock.

Since 1947, a Catholic Church committee has examined 1,300 claims and presented 29 to the Church - 19 were recognized as miracles.

The reason most claims were not recognized is due to no original diagnosis or medications also being taken. To the person healed these objections are irrelevant of course.

But every pilgrim, sick or well, feels strengthened and spiritually refreshed from a pilgrimage.

Another revelation is how helping other pilgrims along the way connects one with self-healing.

A pilgrimage is a metaphor for life; your journey on earth in miniature.

Lessons learned and transformations become part of who you are...

Q
is for
QUMRAN

"For those who believe, no words are necessary. For those who do not believe, no words are possible." Saint Ignasius of Loyola

By the early Middle Ages, the Church had concluded that Mary Magdalene was a redeemed prostitute.

This seems to result from her being identified as the unnamed woman and sinner who anointed Jesus's feet in the Gospel of Luke.

At that time, a *sinner* was not synonymous with *prostitute*, and so it is surprising that Pope Gregory the Great pronounced this view in 591, and it became official Catholic teaching.

Despite this, Mary Magdalene emerged as being the most popular saint during the Middle Ages, highly praised by the church as a model of repentance.

However, a discovery made in the Middle East in the 1940's would turn Christian teachings on its head.

Qumran is an archaeological site in the West Bank near the Israeli settlement and kibbutz of Kalya. Many scholars believe the location was home to a Jewish sect, probably the Essenes.

Explorers first came across *Qumran* in the 19th century, and the site took on new importance with the discovery of the Dead Sea Scrolls in 1947.

Over the next decade, local Bedouin and scientific researchers would discover the remains of more than 900 manuscripts in 11 caves.

Carbon dating indicates they were penned roughly between 200BC and 70AD.

Documents had also been found in Upper Egypt...

In 1945, fifty-two papyrus texts, including gospels and other secret documents, were found concealed in an earthenware jar buried near Nag Hammadi in the Egyptian desert.

A young Arab shepherd called Muhammed Edh-Dhib was looking for a stray goat.

Amusing himself by throwing stones at a rock, one of them fell down a hole and he heard a 'clink' as it hit a pottery jar containing parchment.

The account of how these documents travelled from the nomadic tribesmen who found them, through the black markets - one of the papyrus books even found its way into the hands of Carl Jung, and eventually back to Cairo, would make a good book on its own!

These Gnostic writings were Coptic translations from the original Greek. They included poems, quasi-philosophical descriptions of the origins of the universe, myths, magic and instructions for mystic practice.

They were later declared heretical as they offered a powerful alternative to the Orthodox Christian tradition and Gnosticism were stamped out.

These Christian texts portrayed Mary Magdalene in a very different light; as a teacher, healer and a leader in the Christian community - even as an incarnation of Sophia, the Goddess of Wisdom.

The Church rescinded their declaration in 1969; but Mary Magdalene is firmly imprinted in our collective consciousness as a sinner turned devoted follower of Jesus.

Mary Magdalene was the first person to see Jesus resurrected from the tomb.

Jesus then sent her to announce the Resurrection to the apostles fulfilling her role as *Apostle to the Apostles*.

In recognition of this, in June 2016, the Vatican council declared the celebration of Saint Mary Magdalene was to be elevated to the level of a feast day *"to stress the importance of this woman, who shows great love for Christ and was very dear to Christ".*

We are hearing countless legends of Mary Magdalene throughout Europe passed down through oral tradition.

Accounts of her marriage to Jesus, mothering a daughter and travels to Europe are no longer *skeletons in the cupboard* and being openly discussed by both lay people and scholars.

R

RATU BAGUS

"Gratitude is not only the greatest of virtues, but the parent of all others." Cicero (106-43BC)

Ratu Bagus is an Energy Master who lives and teaches Bio-Energy Meditation or Shaking Yoga on his ashram in Bali, at the foothills of Mount Agung, a sacred volcano. Bali is beautiful and deserves its title as "Island of the Gods".

Although not directly related to Mary Magdalene, my experiences at the ashram with Ratu have been stepping stones (boulders actually!) in my life; I would not be writing this book without the guidance and encouragement I have received from him.

Ratu means 'queen' and Bagus means 'good' in Indonesian.

This meditation practice connects us with our soul and with nature.

Ratu helps us to clear blocks, physical, mental and or emotional, which prevent us from living a healthy and happy life.

I was introduced to him in Dorset in November 2004.

I literally saw God in his face - unconditional love.

I was a practising Christian and had, and still have, a close connection with Jesus. But he is not here in the flesh, and I wanted guidance from a living teacher.

I have been a regular visitor to his ashram since my first visit in April 2005.

Ratu has taught me many things but the most important message is for us to love ourselves, to be positive, active and creative. To eat light, breathe deep and laugh long - to be happy! Simple but not always easy!

It has been an incredible journey of self-discovery and I have made many friends through this practice. They are my shaking family - we have laughed and cried together, but more laughter than tears!

We have a local group who meets once a week in Avebury, a chance to reconnect in the Heart of England with Ratu, myself and my friends. It is an oasis...

Ratu never refers to himself as a guru. He wants us all to be our own teacher.

He is a human being with divine gifts and his mission is to serve humanity for as long as he lives and breathes.

For this dedication and commitment he has my utmost respect and appreciation.

www.ratubagus.com

R

REINCARNATION

I have included a second entry for R as a central tenet of this book is my belief in reincarnation or rebirth.

That after each biological death we start a new life in a different physical body.

If you are not open to this, nothing I have written makes sense!

All major religions subscribe to this, namely Buddhism, Hinduism, Jainism and Sikhism.

Greek philosophers such as Pythagoras, Socrates and Plato believed in rebirth.

Mainstream Christians and Islamists do not believe we reincarnate, but groups within do; followers of Kabbalah, the Cathars, Alawites, the Druze and the Rosicrucians.

Scientists do not accept reincarnation due to lack of empirical evidence!

Or maybe they are reluctant to admit their scientific theories and methods of investigation have limitations? Or just outdated?

But there is plenty of anecdotal evidence... Close to home...

I was a church going Christian; my ordered, scientific view of the world was shattered by a 2 year old, my own son!

Not unusual for a 2 year old, he was having a tantrum in his bedroom shouting

"I want to go home!"
I held him until he calmed down, and then quietly said to him

"But you are home."

He just looked at me with his green eyes, slowly shaking his head from side to side.

I felt shocked to the core. In an instant I had been transformed from his mother to a vehicle who had brought him into this world. My ego didn't like it one bit.

This happened several times and gave me a strange feeling and reminder that this child did not belong to me - rather he was on loan from God.

It dawned on me that I could learn a lot from this chid, but I didn't want to probe.

When he turned 3, he was able to express himself better.

On one occasion when he was not complying with my wishes, I said he ought to be nice to me because he only had one mummy (I shudder when I write this).

"No, I have two mummies." he replied in a dead pan fashion.

Well that stopped me in my tracks!

I took a deep breath and turning to him I said

"Thank you for choosing me and daddy. I feel privileged to be your mummy."

He looked at me and said nothing. Silence is powerful!

Part of me wanted to relate my experiences with my special son, and another part wanted to protect him and grow up as a normal child.

So I wrote it down in my journal, and have waited until he is an adult - he is 21 now (a normal sport loving, beer drinking history student!)

My husband was 58 when our son was born and he has always been acutely aware of his mortality.

On the way to nursery school one morning, he turned to me and said

"When I grow up will Daddy be big or small?"

I wasn't sure what he meant, so without trying to put words into his mouth I replied,

"Do you mean will Daddy be a grown up or spirit?"

He nodded in agreement with a very serious expression on his face.

I replied I didn't know.

I own my imperfections as a mother (like the coercive control earlier!), but I have always tried to be honest to my children.

And I expected the same from them, even though it wasn't always what I wanted to hear!

I went onto say it was natural for Daddy and I to die before him - hopefully he would have his own family by them.

He then said he hoped he would get me as a Mummy next time.

Nothing like planning ahead. He went on

"Will Daddy be your husband in the next world too?"

Good question...

Here are some of his comments made on the school run during

his preschool years (3-5 years old):-
"Heaven is a really fun place because God is with you and you are never lonely"

"Heaven is dark but not scary because God is there"

"Nothing dies Mummy, your spirit goes on for ever!"

"I don't want to die because I don't want to leave you Mummy"

Out of the mouths of babes...

I have always said I have learnt more from my children than all the books I have read!

I owe them everything...

This is where my 'spiritual' journey began (in this lifetime anyway!)

US psychiatrist Ian Stevenson investigated many reports of young children who remember a past life.

 He conducted more than 2,500 case studies over a period of 40 years and published 12 books including

"Children who Remember Previous Lives: A Question of Reincarnation"

Sceptics dismiss the reports as 'anecdotal', but the way my son spoke to me was deadly serious and he was definitely speaking his truth.

Just because he is a child why should his truth be less valid?

One could argue as a child from God (as we all were), he is less tainted by the world and therefore more reliable!

S

is for
SACRED UNION

"Life is Divine, life is an extraordinary, incredible, miraculous phenomenon, our most precious gift." Robert Muller

Sacred Union is natural to humans, as we are trying to return to Oneness or God - the ocean of spirit we originated from.

However, before we enter into relationship with a partner, we need to find Sacred Relationship or wholeness within ourselves.

One of the reasons there are difficulties within relationships today is that many have not found the wholeness in themselves and are looking for it in a partner to make them whole.

Without this Divine element sexual union is purely a release of tension.

Ultimately this can never work.

If we find union within ourselves by balancing the Masculine and the Feminine and therefore union with God, we can come to a relationship *full.*

Then we have *love* and *light* to offer a partner.

Sexuality is a Divine gift, a sacrament of love, a divine method of union with the Divine.

Men and women who follow this path are known as the "Carriers of the Flame".

In the ancient scriptures, we are told that God has also become separated into two parts, one masculine and one feminine.

The process of *Sacred Union* is where two lovers merge into One; in addition to the full reunion of God the Father with God the Mother, the two human beings experience rapturous union with an explosion of orgasmic Light.

Throughout the ages, *Sacred Union* has been known by many names such as *Hieros Gamos* in Christianity, *Yab-Yum* in Tibetan Buddhism and *Sacred Marriage* in the Kabbalah.

The foundation of *Sacred Union* would involve the uniting and merging of Love, Power and Wisdom through sexuality, the heart and consciousness.

A Sacred partnership is a form of alchemy, bringing love and light to the world, greater than the two could bring as individuals. This is Sacred Alchemy.

The reunion of Twin Souls is the coalescence of God.

You shall know your Twin Soul (Beloved) by the way he/she makes you feel.

There will be a quality of deep trust, passion, longing, gratitude and unspeakable happiness.

Some historical examples of human beings who have entered this sacred union:-

King Solomon and the Queen of Sheba, Isis and Osiris, Sophia and The Logos.

The most recent couple in history and relevant here is Jesus and Mary Magdalene...

Jesus was ahead of his time.

He wanted to raise and embrace the feminine in his Sacred Union with Mary Magdalene, restoring the balance of masculine and feminine energies to earth.

"As it is on Heaven shall it be on Earth..."

As above so below...

T
is for
TANTRA

"The truest nature of anything is the highest it can become."
Aristotle

Tantrism is a movement within both Hinduism and Buddhism combining magical and mystical elements together with sacred writings known as The Tantra.

In the Indian tradition Tantra is synonymous with kundalini yoga.

In Egyptian tradition it was known as the Sex Magic of Isis, or the Alchemy of Horus, depending on whether it was practiced with a partner or solo.

Sexual energy can be directed in specific ways through breathing and visualization techniques to reach a higher level of being and a sustained feeling of ecstasy which gives us a glimpse of what it feels like to be connected to our Divine source.

Mary Magdalene would have been trained in The Tantra during her time in Egypt. This would have included meditation practices and sexual magic, the secrets of which she would have shared with Jesus to strengthen his etheric (subtle) body.

Yab-yum (see above) is a classic tantric image of a masculine God in union with a feminine God, seated in the meditative pose known as yab-yum.

Yab-yum represents the mystical union of wisdom (feminine) and compassion (masculine).

Union and polarity is a central teaching in Tantric Buddhism.

The union is realized by the practitioner as a mystical experience within one's own body.

The God and Goddess or Mother-Father God - Divine or Sacred union of the Masculine and the Feminine.

As above so below...

U

is for

UNITY BREATH

"Your sacred space is where you can find yourself again and again." J Campbell

Before any important ceremony, indigenous people of the world believe they must connect in love with Mother Earth, Father Sky, and Great Spirit or God.

This is known as *The Unity Breath* and Drunvalo Melchizedek explains it beautifully in his book *"Living in the Heart"*.

This is what I do before I meditate:-

I love the seaside so I imagine myself walking along a white sandy beach with the surf lapping at my ankles and a warm breeze flowing through my hair.

I visualize my love into a small sphere and send it down to 'Mother Earth'.

I wait for her to send it back to me and I breathe it up through my feet and let it permeate every cell in my body, finally filling my heart.

Maintaining that connection, I turn my attention to Father Sky, the stars, the Moon and the mighty Sun, sustainer of life on our planet.

I feel its warmth and brilliance shining down on me.

I send a sphere of love to the Sun and wait for a shower of light to enter my body through my crown. This travels around my body and finally in my heart.

Now the Divine Mother and Divine Father are joined with me in pure love, and I, the Divine child, complete the triangle.

I drop down into my heart and say to myself *'Let there be Light'*.

Then, with intention, I go into the tiny sacred space of my heart.

From this place, you can create what you want in your life.

For example, I would like a place by the sea. I have a picture of a cottage overlooking a sandy beach pinned to my bathroom mirror. I look at this twice a day when I am cleaning my teeth!

I see this image in my sacred space. I feel the sun on my face, the wind in my hair and the smell of the sea.

I *know* this will manifest in the next two years. I wrote a list of three requests on a post-it last year and look at it before I go to sleep. I have already ticked the first two!

I have friends whose lives have changed dramatically using the same techniques.

Start with something small, to gain confidence and work up to bigger things.

The Universe only acts in your highest interest so put your intention out and try to detach from it.

Trust and let go!

V

VESICA PISCIS

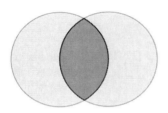

"If you miss the moment, you miss your life." John Daido Loori

God was symbolized as a circle in the earliest cultures, having no beginning or end.

The creation of a second circle symbolized the start of the duality of god and goddess, male and female.

When two circles of equal radius intersect, the almond shaped *Vesica Piscis* is formed as if the god and goddess created a divine offspring.

The *Vesica Piscis* design and its offshoots, the Flower of Life, Tree of Life, and fundamentals of geometry, go back thousands of years preceding nearly all today's religions.

The *vessel of the fish* is an archetypal symbol of the Goddess of love and fertility known as the *womb* and *doorway to life*.

The *Vesica Piscis* has feminine associations with the bridal chamber and Holy of Holies (*hieros gamos*).

The *Vesica Piscis* has great significance; the union of heaven and earth in the body of Christ; the merging of God and Goddess, the yoni or vagina of the female goddess, the root element of the Flower of Life in sacred geometry, square roots and harmonic dimensions.

The *Vesica Piscis* represents the Pythagorean 'measure of the fish', or junction of the physical and spiritual world.

With one end extended to look like the tail of a fish, it was used as a simple 'fish' symbol for early Christian faith.

In fact it still is...

The *Vesica Piscis* can be found on nearly every medieval church in Europe.

Many of these churches were devoted to the Virgin Mary or to Mary Magdalene...

The Chapel of St Mary in Glastonbury (also called Avalon, the island of the Goddess) is decorated with the *Vesica Piscis*.

In the photograph left, the lid of the Chalice Well at Glastonbury is decorated with a *Vesica Piscis* iron grid.

 W

WAY OF THE HEART

"Look within. Be still. Free from fear and attachment, know the sweet joy of the way." Buddha

The *Way of the Heart* is the only way forward...

Get out of your heads/minds and live in your heart!

Our minds are useful to run our day to day lives, but the mind should be the *president* and not the *dictator*!

The amount of time and energy we spend in our heads, brooding and worrying, makes it difficult for us to receive inner guidance.

Let go of the judgement and worry, and relax into the peace of your heart.

Here you are calm and peaceful, open to guidance and inspiration at any time.

When I first went to Ratu's ashram I was frightened of *losing my mind!*

That fear held me back for so long...

Ratu said I was frightened of my own power - my Divine Feminine power!

Mary Magdalene has given me the courage to finally sit down and write this...

I can't stop thinking about her!
I wake up in the night and she makes suggestions, ideas 'pop' into my head as to what I should write!

I get up early - she is urging me on...

This book is like an evolving organism...

Love, compassion, forgiveness and blessing are the qualities she speaks with when I hear my inner voice.

She is waiting in the wings for *all* of us - you just have to invite her in!

X is for
THE GREEK LETTER X OR CHI

In Greek, the language of the New Testament, the word Christos (Christ) begins with the letter *"X"* or *chi*. It became the early Christian symbol for Christos (Christ).

A *Christogram* is a monogram that forms an abbreviation for the name of Jesus Christ.

One of the oldest Christograms is the *Chi-Rho*.

It consists of the superimposed Greek letters chi (X) and rho (P) shown above, which are the first two letters of the Greek word for "Christ".

It was displayed in the labarum military standard used by Constantine in AD 312.

These two letters became a shorthand for Christ.

This has been shortened to just the letter X, as in Xmas.

There is a common misconception that the word Xmas stems from a secular attempt to remove the religious tradition from Christmas by taking the "Christ" out of "Christmas", but its use dates back to the 16th century.

It became a favourite symbol of an alternative medieval church who honoured her as Domina.

Double X's were an important symbol for these Christians who honoured the Sacred Feminine, and often occur among their watermarks.

Placed side-by-side and touching, the X's form XX, the intertwined A and V symbols used to represent Ave Maria and Ave Millennium, two of their significant slogans.

After the Inquisition in 1239 when thousands of Cathars were murdered in France in an attempt to eradicate the rumours about Jesus and Mary Magdalene, the heresy was taken up by the art world.

The letter "X" appeared in watermarks, paintings and tapestries.

Often the artists did not supply titles to their paintings, leaving it to viewers to identify a scene or character by symbolism.

The letter "X shows up in numerous paintings of Mary Magdalene, either on her clothes or in church windows.

Y

"To err is human, to forgive Divine." Alexander Pope (1688-1744)

Yeshua (as Mary Magdalene called him) was an ardent feminist and it is no wonder women from all walks of life left their homes to follow him.

At that time women were 'second class citizens' and husbands viewed them as property.

They must have been astonished when *Yeshua* cured the woman with the continual menstrual flow who reached out to touch his robe as he passed by; (a Jewish woman would not be allowed to touch a Jewish man) - she represented the unclean status of women in their society.

The casting out of the seven demons by *Yeshua* is the first time we meet Mary Magdalene in the Bible.

At that time the number seven possessed great power and significance.

Seven days of creation, seven notes in an octave, seven colours in a rainbow, seven energy centres or chakras, seven endocrine glands in the body.

It is the basis of all life.

The Pythagoreans called it the *perfect number* and it is the most frequently mentioned number in the Bible.

The ancients watched the seven visible planets moving across the background of 'fixed stars'.

The seven planetary Gods; Moon, Mercury, Venus, Sun, Mars, Jupiter and Saturn were where they thought souls ascended in order to reach perfection.

So the 'healing' of Mary Magdalene may have been an initiation into completeness and perfection; rather different to what the Gospels led us to believe!

My *cellular memory* confirms this to be the case...

No wonder she understood *Yeshua* more than the male disciples!

Z is for
ZERO POINT FIELD

"Sit down before fact like a little child, and be prepared to give up every preconceived notion, follow humbly wherever, to whatever abyss Nature leads, or you shall learn nothing"
T.H. Huxley (1825-1895)

There is a background sea of quantum energy in the universe - *zero point energy.*

Zero is, simultaneously, both the smallest and the largest number.

It is nothing, and it is everything. It is both empty and full.

A *paradox.*

The *zero point field* did not fit with *Newtonian* physics – these equations work well for sending rockets to the moon but do not work with subatomic particles.

They believed the effect of the *zero point field* was insignificant, so they ignored the *zero point field* and it remained largely unknown for nearly 100 years!

It has been brought to the public's attention largely due to scientific journalist Lynn McTaggart and her book *'The Field'*.

Meticulously researched, it chronicles the history and discoveries made in quantum physics to the layman, where credited scientists have been investigating paranormal phenomena such as remote viewing, telepathy and distance healing in laboratory conditions.

Zero point energy is now used to explain the *Heisenberg uncertainty principle,* where one cannot know the position and speed of a subatomic particle at the same time. Randomly virtual photons jump back and forth in a cosmic dance between the zero point field and our physical world.

These particles are called *virtual* as they are not stable enough to stay in our reality.

The continuous flow of energy in and out of the material world resembles what Eastern Hindu cosmology described as the cosmic dance of Shiva.

All of our outcomes exist in energetic potential and even a *small* change can dramatically change our destiny!

The future is not something that *happens.* It is something we create.

Yes, there are elements and influences beyond us.

The laws of nature and our own nature constrain our choices...

And there are great catastrophes, earthquakes, plagues and floods that constrain our choices.

But it means we can reclaim our power, determining what we create in every present moment.

In addition, matter is not *solid* but a form of energy.

We are all light emitting forms of energy.

Scientists are now able to measure zero point energy; one cup of zero point energy is enough to bring all the oceans of the world to boiling point!

Physical reality is made up of an infinite field of energy and information.

The Universe is a type of hologram!

The principle of the hologram is that each part contains within it the information that codes for the whole, that is, all information exists non-locally, infinitely reflected in all the facets of existence.

This theory was pioneered by David Bohm, a former student of Einstein, and the quantum physicist Karl Pribram.

The holographic model explains paranormal events such as telepathy, out-of-body experiences, synchronicity, "lucid" dreaming and even mystical traditions such as cosmic unity and miraculous healings.

Why is science so resistant to the paranormal?

Yale surgeon, Dr Bernie Siegel, author of "*Love, Medicine and Miracles*", asserts it is because people are addicted to their beliefs.

Siegel says this is why when you try to change someone's belief they act like an addict.

The research of the Global Consciousness Project (GCP) has yielded irrefutable proof of the link between the zero point field and processes occurring within the collective human mind on earth.

The GCP has set up all around the globe (65 in 2007) random number generators (RNG's) whose data is fed into the internet and linked back to Princeton University.

In data from four hours before the September 11 terrorist attacks, they found an enormous level of coherence between the RNG's, indicating a global *forewarning* of a large impending event.

The period immediately surrounding the event shows a huge spike in coherence as humanity's collective mind was focused consciously on events as they unfolded.

The same results occurred before the Asian tsunami of 2004 and during the funeral service of Princess Diana.

The GCP has proven that consciousness is a real something; it can *see* into the near future and collective consciousness focused in harmony can affect quantum events.

This suggests consciousness focused in harmony is more fundamental than any form of energy/matter in space-time.

If thought equals energy and energy equals matter, then thoughts become matter!

Mind over quantum matter!

We are co-creating our own world and we are all connected.

So what can we do?

What should we focus on?

Instead of bemoaning the horrors and corruption within our political and financial institutions, emitting anger and resentment into the world, we should focus on the here and now on what we want to manifest in the world.

As Ghandi said *"Be the change you wish to see in the world"*.

Transforming our world from the illusion of separation, by bringing the joy and peace of the *furthest* reaches of heaven into even the *tiniest* moments of our everyday lives - surely that is our challenge and the Holy Grail of today?

EPILOGUE

"Without myth, however, every culture loses its healthy, creative power: it is only a horizon encompassed with myth that rounds off to unity a social movement." Friedrich Nietzche (1844-1900)

The many faces of Mary Magdalene will remain a mystery as we are unable to fully unveil her through written records.

Until the mysteries of quantum science are unravelled, the story of Mary Magdalene will remain just that, a story, and opinion will remain divided on her.

Whether or not she was a former prostitute, married to Jesus and bore his child are not important to her now, that was all in the past, and she has let it go...

Off the record, my *cellular memory* tells me she was a highly intelligent and beautiful woman with auburn hair and dark brown eyes.

She was 26 years old when she met Jesus and was *indeed* a *high-class* prostitute (this would explain her independent wealth and ability to fund Jesus' mission).

Mary Magdalene and Jesus were not married; it was a *spiritual* or *sacred union*.

After the crucifixion, Mary Magdalene and her inner circle returned to the temple school in Alexandria, Egypt where she had trained before she met Jesus.

Here she gave birth to Sarah, the fruit of her union with Jesus.

She and her companions travelled to France by boat in AD43 where she lived for the next twenty years. She died in AD 63 at the age of 56.

All this information is in the *Akashic Records* and accessible to each and every one of you.

I realise these words will not be well received by many and I will be ridiculed and rejected by some, but with Mary Magdalene walking with me every step of the way, I have spoken my truth and fulfilled my part of the bargain by putting pen to paper.

If what I say is true and we are all part of an interconnected cosmic dance, this message is already out in the world!

The discussion about Mary Magdalene has brought her back into our consciousness and enables her to fulfil her role in present day.

As I said earlier we have moved from the Age of Pisces into the Age of Aquarius, the age of equality between the Masculine and Feminine.

Mary Magdalene has been called to support this process, so the Divine Feminine can step forward and assume her rightful place beside the Divine Masculine.

This is for all women and men, as we all contain the Divine Feminine and Divine Masculine.

The Feminine brings life energy, love, vitality, wisdom, faith, receptivity to the Divine, feeling and inclusivity.

The Masculine brings insight, understanding, awareness, goal-setting and implementation of the Divine plan.

We all contain both, we just need a balance, so we can all experience the joys of life in a cosmic dance with the Divine and one another.

As we imbue a feeling of "all is one" deep in our hearts, we can express our innate gifts and co-create life in a conscious, beneficial way to all mankind.

Mary Magdalene will be in our midst until this process is complete.

AFTERWORD

Long buried and suppressed, the Gnostic Gospels contain the secret writings of the followers of Jesus.

One of Mary Magdalene's icons is a book; thought to signify her role as guardian of the mysteries imparted by Jesus.

I think it is much more significant...

My cellular memory tells me she was involved in the writing of these texts.

If my theory is correct, that she sought asylum in Alexandria, Egypt after the crucifixion, at the school she trained at before she met Jesus…

What did she do for the next nine years?

She was writing…

Where were the texts discovered? Egypt.

Coincidence?

I don't believe in them!

This is what she wants me to write about next..

To serve you is a blessing and my privilege.

I send you all love and light and wish you well on your journeys.

BIBLIOGRAPHY

The author wishes to thank all those whose invaluable work is listed below:-

Emoto, Dr M	The Hidden Messages of Water, *Atria 2005.*
Haskins, S	Mary Magdalene: Myth & Metaphor, *Harcourt Brace 1994.*
Heinemann, K & G	Orbs: Their Mission and Messages of Hope, *Hay House 2010.*
Houston, Siobhan	Invoking Mary Magdalene, *Sounds True Inc 2006.*
Jacobs, A	Gnostic Gospels, *Watkins Publishing 2016.* Gospel of Judas, Mary Magdalene & Thomas
Jung, C G	Answer to Job, *Routledge 2002.*
Kirkel, M	Mary Magdalene Beckons, *Into the Heart Creations 2012.*
Lipton, Bruce H PhD	The Biology of Belief, *Cygnus Books 2005.*
Loup, J	The Gospel of Mary Magdalene, *Inner Traditions 2002.*
McTaggart, L	The Field, *Element 2003.*
Melchizedek, D	Living in the Heart, *Light Technology Publishing 2003.*
Siegel, Dr B	Love, Medicine & Miracles, *Rider 1999.*
Starbird, M	Mary Magdalene - Bride in Exile, *Bear & Company 2005.*
Sylvia, C & Novak W	A Change of Heart, *Grand Central Publishing 1998.*
Talbot, M	The Holographic Universe, *Harper Collins 1991.*
Taylor, S A	The Akashic Records, *Hay House 2016.*
Welborn, A	Mary Magdalene: Truth, Legends & Lies, *Kindle 2017.*